First Facts®

Christmas around the World

Christmas in
FRANCE

by Jack Manning

raintree
a Capstone company — publishers for children

Raintree is an imprint of Capstone Global Library Limited, a company incorporated in England and Wales having its registered office at 264 Banbury Road, Oxford, OX2 7DY – Registered company number: 6695582

www.raintree.co.uk
myorders@raintree.co.uk

Brenda Haugen, editor; Gene Bentdahl, designer; Eric Gohl, media researcher;
Jennifer Walker, production specialist

ISBN 978 1 4747 2573 6
20 19 18 17 16
10 9 8 7 6 5 4 3 2 1

British Library Cataloguing in Publication Data
A full catalogue record for this book is available from the British Library.

Acknowledgements
We would like to thank the following for permission to reproduce photographs: Capstone Studio: Karon Dubke, 21; Dreamstime: Claudio Momberto, 6, Giancarlo Liguori, 5; Fotolia: Marco Desscouleurs, 1; Newscom: Godong/picture-alliance/Fred de Noyelle, 11, 17, PHOTOPQR/ L'UNION DE REIMS/Christian Philippe, 15, ZUMA Press/Colorise/Risler, 12, ZUMA Press/ Stephane Geufroi, 20; Shutterstock: pearl7, 18; Super Stock Inc.: Photononstop, cover, 8.
Design elements: Shutterstock.

Every effort has been made to contact copyright holders of material reproduced in this book. Any omissions will be rectified in subsequent printings if notice is given to the publisher.

All the internet addresses (URLs) given in this book were valid at the time of going to press. However, due to the dynamic nature of the internet, some addresses may have changed, or sites may have changed or ceased to exist since publication. While the author and publisher regret any inconvenience this may cause readers, no responsibility for any such changes can be accepted by either the author or the publisher.

Made in China

CONTENTS

Christmas in France

People sing songs. Flowers fill homes with colour. Children write letters asking for gifts. These are some of the sights and sounds of Christmas in France. People celebrate Christmas Day on 25 December. But the Christmas season lasts much longer. It begins on 6 December with the feast of Saint Nicholas. Christmas celebrations end on 6 January with Epiphany.

How to say it!

In France people say *"Joyeux Noël"*, which means "Happy Christmas".

France

CHRISTMAS FACT!

Christians believe that three kings followed a star to the stable where Jesus was born. The kings brought gifts for Jesus. Epiphany celebrates the day the three kings first saw Jesus.

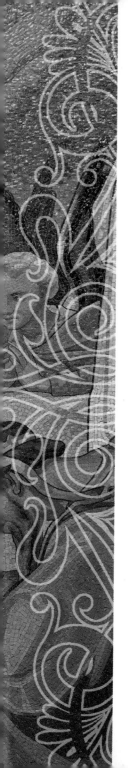

The first Christmas

Christmas is a **Christian** festival that celebrates the birth of Jesus. Christians believe that long ago, Mary and Joseph travelled to the town of Bethlehem. Mary was going to have a baby. When Mary and Joseph got to the city, they had nowhere to stay. They spent the night in a stable. Jesus was born there.

Christian person who follows a religion based on the teachings of Jesus. Christians believe that Jesus is the son of God.

Christmas celebrations

The Christmas season is full of celebrations. The feast of Saint Nicholas starts the season. Saint Nicholas helped poor children. On his feast day, children often receive chocolate or other treats.

Most people celebrate on Christmas Eve. They go to midnight church services. A meal called *réveillon* follows the services. *Réveillon* means to wake up.

The last day of the Christmas season is Epiphany: Three Kings Day. Many people go to church on Epiphany. They also eat a special treat called the Cake of Kings.

Christmas symbols

The nativity is a symbol of Christmas. It is a scene that reminds people of Jesus' birth.

Many nativity scenes include small figures called *santons*. Most santons look like people or animals. Some represent Jesus, Mary and Joseph. Others are shaped like the three kings.

Santons are made from hard, waterproof clay. Many people paint their santons by hand.

Christmas decorations

Flowers decorate many tables during the Christmas season. Roses, carnations and snapdragons are popular choices.

People decorate their homes with Christmas trees. They sometimes use potted trees, which can be planted outside after the Christmas season.

People put **ornaments** and lights on their Christmas trees. Common ornaments include baubles, bells and angels.

ornament decoration hung on a Christmas tree

Father Christmas

Most French children believe
in Père Noël, which means Father
Christmas. Père Noël is a tall man
with a white beard. He wears a long,
red robe. He carries a sack of gifts
for children.

Children write letters to Père
Noël at the North Pole. In the letters,
children politely ask for gifts.

CHRISTMAS FACT!

A donkey sometimes helps Père Noël carry his sack. Many children leave out snacks for Père Noël and his donkey on Christmas Eve.

Christmas presents

Some people believe Père Noël comes twice. He brings small gifts and chocolate for children on the feast of Saint Nicholas. Père Noël also comes on Christmas Eve.

Some children put their shoes near the fireplace on Christmas Eve. Others put their shoes near the nativity or the Christmas tree. They hope Père Noël will fill them with presents.

Children open their gifts on Christmas Day. Adults open their gifts on New Year's Eve. Most children receive toys, games and chocolate.

CHRISTMAS FACT!

Many people give gifts to people in their community who provide services, such as the local butcher.

Many people once burned large logs called yule logs. Now, many people eat cakes shaped like yule logs.

Christmas food

On Christmas Eve families gather around tables filled with food. They eat small helpings from the many dishes. The meal may last for hours.

People eat many different foods during the Christmas season. Some eat roast goose. Others eat turkey and chestnuts. **Oysters** are a favourite Christmas food in Paris, the capital of France.

oyster edible shellfish

Christmas songs

Christmas in France is a joyful time filled with music. One famous Christmas song from France is "Oh, Holy Night".

Many people celebrate Christmas with musical shows. The shows are held in churches, concert halls and theatres.

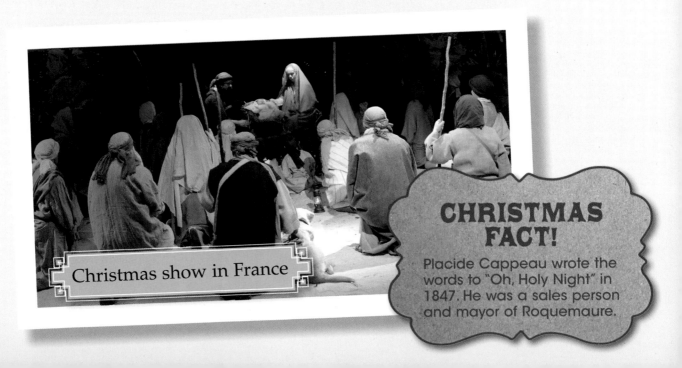

Christmas show in France

CHRISTMAS FACT!

Placide Cappeau wrote the words to "Oh, Holy Night" in 1847. He was a sales person and mayor of Roquemaure.

Hands-on:
MAKE A KING

The three kings came to a stable in Bethlehem to see the baby Jesus. Now you can make your own king to decorate your home.

What you need

- construction paper in several colours
- glue
- scissors
- coloured pencils or felt-tip pens

What to do

1. Roll a sheet of construction paper into a tube, and glue it in place.
2. After the glue has dried, cut out two squares about 2.5 centimetres (1 inch) high on opposite sides of the bottom of the tube. These cut-outs will form the king's legs.
3. Make the king's face from a strip of construction paper that is a different colour from the tube. Use coloured pencils or felt-tip pens to draw the king's eyes, nose and mouth. Glue the face around the top of the tube.
4. Create a beard by cutting slits along the bottom edge of another strip of construction paper. Glue the beard to the tube beneath the king's mouth.
5. Make a crown for your king with another strip of construction paper. Cut points along the top of the paper to make the crown. Then glue the crown in place.
6. Decorate your king. You can add cut-outs or draw designs on your king and his crown.

GLOSSARY

Christian person who follows a religion based on the teachings of Jesus. Christians believe that Jesus is the son of God.

ornament decoration hung on a Christmas tree

oyster edible shellfish

READ MORE

Big Book of Christmas Decorations to Cut, Fold and & Stick, Fiona Watt (Usborne Publishing Ltd, 2013)

Christmas (Holidays and Festivals), Nancy Dickmann (Raintee, 2011)

Room for a Little One: The Story of Christmas, Martin Waddell (Orchard Books, 2015)

WEBSITE

www.bbc.co.uk/languages/christmas/french/

Discover Christmas traditions in France!

INDEX